"Using his renowned teaching skills, Alistair uses this book not only to instruct us how to pray but to show how our prayers reveal what we believe about God. Read this to learn who you are speaking to and what you need to say to him. Get ready to have your prayer life radically changed."

JANET PARSHALL, Host, *In the Market With Janet Parshall*

"I love this book. It comes from the heart of a seasoned pastor to the hearts of men and women who desperately need help in our prayers. I was challenged and convicted, and yet also moved to devotion to God and to a fresh conviction of the wonder of the gospel of the Lord Jesus. There is a rich combination of scriptural clarity and pastoral warmth. And I love the way the book is laced with hymns, songs and poems, too!"

CHRISTOPHER ASH, Writer-in-residence, Tyndale House, Cambridge, UK; Author, *Zeal Without Burnout*

"For most of us, the discipline of prayer is the hardest one to master. That means we need more motivation and more instruction to strengthen our resolve. I am thankful that Alistair provides both for us in *Pray Big*. Here is a book that can reignite your heart in prayer."

JOHN MACARTHUR, Pastor, Grace Community Church, Sun Valley, California; President, The Master's Seminary

"On the morning after I began reading this book, I found that my own personal prayer life had been enriched and deepened by Alistair's challenge that we 'pray big' by imitating the apostle Paul's God-exalting, God-trusting, God-glorifying pattern of prayer for the Ephesian churches. This is a wise, practical, biblically-faithful book. It will deepen your prayer life!"

WAYNE GRUDEM, Distinguished Research Professor of Theology and Biblical Studies, Phoenix Seminary, Arizona

"One of the most influential and engaging authors of our time has done it again with *Pray Big*. Pastor Alistair Begg speaks from his heart, guiding us into a much more knowledgeable, meaningful, and powerful prayer life. This book is a must-read for all of us."

DAVID KIM, Concertmaster, The Philadelphia Orchestra

"Here is a nourishing book where each short chapter will stir your heart to pray bigger prayers. If you are feeling that your prayer times are stale and discouraging, this biblical and experiential book will reform and refresh."

PAUL REES, Lead Pastor, Charlotte Chapel, Edinburgh

"This is a delightfully warm-hearted, crystal-clear encouragement to bask in the gospel, and to pray in a way which fits with who we are in Christ. This book made me want to 'pray big'—which is exactly the point!"

GARY MILLAR, Principal, Queensland Theological College, Australia

"We will be forever grateful to Alistair for how he helped us understand and apply Christian basics to every facet of life and worship, and there is nothing more basic and transformational than prayer. There is no greater challenge for the Western church than to be a praying people; so we are thrilled and grateful for this vital book."

KEITH AND KRISTYN GETTY, Hymnwriters; Authors, *Sing!*

"Prayer is so important, and so difficult, that we always need more good books on prayer. Alistair writes with a biblical simplicity and pastoral sincerity that will help you not just feel like you *should* pray, but feel that you *can*."

KEVIN DEYOUNG, Senior Pastor, Christ Covenant Church, Matthews, North Carolina; Author, *Crazy Busy*

"This wonderful book will help us to refocus our prayers to pray as God tells us he wants us to pray in the Bible. I found it both liberating and enabling. I am motivated to pray more, and to pray for the right things."

WILLIAM TAYLOR, Rector, St Helen's Bishopsgate, London

"When we get to heaven, we will finally understand how our smallest and most feeble prayers advanced Christ's kingdom in ways we never dreamed. At that point, I don't want to whine, 'Bother! Why didn't I pray bigger?' This book is your best guide to offering up larger-than-life prayers through which God delights to work!"

JONI EARECKSON TADA, Founder, Joni and Friends International Disability Center

ALISTAIR BEGG

PRAY

Learn to Pray Like an Apostle

BIG

To the memory of T. S. Mooney,
who remembered me daily at "the best place."

Pray Big: *Learn to Pray Like an Apostle*
© Alistair Begg, 2019.
Reprinted 2019, 2020, 2021 (twice), 2022.

Published by:
The Good Book Company

thegoodbook.com | thegoodbook.co.uk
thegoodbook.com.au | thegoodbook.co.nz | thegoodbook.co.in

Published in association with the literary agency of Wolgemuth & Associates, Inc.

ISBN: 9781784983369 | Printed in the UK

Design by André Parker

CONTENTS

INTRODUCTION:
WHO WE PRAY TO

I want to pray bigger, and better. I want you to, too.

Our prayers tell us a great deal about ourselves and our faith. As the nineteenth-century Scottish preacher Robert Murray M'Cheyne reputedly, and memorably, put it:

> *What a man is on his knees before God, that he is, and nothing more.*

Our conversation with others declares what is on our minds. But our conversation with God in private reveals what is in our hearts. Listen to someone pray—or listen to yourself pray—and you gain a window into the very center of the being.

To put it another way: the way we use our money and spend our time reveals a great deal about what are our real priorities and what are our real beliefs. And so do our prayers—whether we pray, for whom we pray, and what we pray.

So how about you, as you read this introduction and decide whether to read on (or whether to buy the book in the first place)? How big are your prayers? Do you ask God for anything? And when you do, are you asking him for big things?

So many of us struggle with prayer. Many books have been written on the subject (and now we can add this one to that long list)—and the reason for that is that prayer doesn't come easy to most of us, in most seasons. And when we do pray, our prayers often seek to do a deal with God; or they are tentative in their requests because we're not sure God will come through; or they are, frankly, so self-centered that they bring little pleasure to the Creator and Savior of the world, as he listens to us present our shopping list of worldly requests to him.

I want to pray bigger, and better. I want you to enjoy praying like that too.

And to do that, we need to discover how to pray as Paul did, which means we need to learn to believe what Paul did. We need to know who we're speaking to, and we need to know what to say to him.

WHO WE SPEAK TO

Paul was a man who knew to whom he was praying. You can meet people who will talk about God in an intellectual way, or a distant way, or a business-like way. But it is distinctly Christian to speak of God as a Father, and to therefore speak to God as a Father. Paul could speak of the grace and peace that come "from God our Father" (Ephesians 1 v 2). The Christian knows that the Creator of everything is not *a* father; he's *their* Father. That's not a metaphor—that's a reality. The apostle John put it this way:

> *See what kind of love the Father has given to us,*
> *that we should be called children of God; and so we*
> *are. (1 John 3 v 1)*

In Galatians Paul puts it wonderfully as he says that...

> *when the fullness of time had come, God sent forth*
> *his Son, born of woman, born under the law, to*
> *redeem those who were under the law, so that we*
> *might receive adoption as sons. And because you*
> *are sons, God has sent the Spirit of his Son into*
> *our hearts, crying "Abba! Father!" So you are no*
> *longer a slave, but a son, and if a son, then an heir*
> *through God. (Galatians 4 v 6-7)*

God sent his Son to make us his sons. God sent his Spirit to enable us to relate to him—to speak to him—as his sons. It is fantastic. That word "Abba" is best translated "Dearest Father." It's the word we find on the lips of Jesus in the Garden of Gethsemane, at his moment of supreme anguish, as he cried out to his Father (Mark 14 v 36; Luke 22 v 41-44).

Paul knew that, through the death and resurrection of his Savior, he knew God as his Father. He understood and enjoyed the great truth that, as Christians, in prayer we do not only approach a majestic Sovereign (though we do) or an impartial Judge (though we do)—we approach our Father in heaven and say, "Dearest Father..."

This is who we speak to when we pray. It's a truth that's easy to understand but equally easy to forget in daily life.

WHAT WE SAY TO HIM

My trouble in prayer is not only that I forget to whom I'm speaking—it's that, often, I'm not really sure what to say. What is it that my Father loves to hear about from me? What is it that I can best pray for my family, my church, and myself?

One of the great privileges of reading the letters of Paul—the first-century apostle, evangelist, church planter and theologian—is that we are allowed to hear the prayers of Paul. We are able to gain a window into the very center of his being, to see what was on his heart. We are able to look in on him not as he is up on his feet, going about the activities of his day, but as he is down on his knees, coming to God in prayer.

This book is not about a doctrine of prayer. It is not a whole theology of prayer. It's not even going to look at all of Paul's prayers. We are going to focus in on Paul's prayers for his friends in the church in Ephesus, which he recounts to them in Ephesians 1 v 15-23 and 3 v 14-21. He's writing to them from prison (though the joy and selflessness that saturate his prayers give no indication of his own predicament). And by explaining what he is praying for them, he's setting them an example for their own prayers—and for ours. The truths that underpin and shape his prayers will motivate us to pray, and they will help us know what to say.

So I am praying that this book will get you praying. You might find it helpful to read one chapter a week, and spend the rest of the week putting Paul's divinely inspired wisdom into practice in your own prayers. Or you could read it at the same time as a friend, and both commit to praying for each other in the ways the apostle lays out.

But whatever you do and however you use this book, be praying that you would pray like Paul—because Paul was a great pray-er. He was confident, he was committed, and he was humble and bold and compassionate. He clearly enjoyed prayer, and was excited about it. He expected his Father in heaven to hear what he said and to act in other people's lives accordingly. He prayed and then was "watchful in it with thanksgiving" (Colossians 4 v 2), ready to see how God would be pleased to answer his prayers.

Paul prayed big prayers because he believed great things. Let's learn from him how we might do the same.

EPHESIANS 1 v 16-21

16 I do not cease to give thanks for you, remembering you in my prayers, 17 that the God of our Lord Jesus Christ, the Father of glory, may give you the Spirit of wisdom and of revelation in the knowledge of him, 18 having the eyes of your hearts enlightened, that you may know what is the hope to which he has called you, what are the riches of his glorious inheritance in the saints, 19 and what is the immeasurable greatness of his power toward us who believe, according to the working of his great might 20 that he worked in Christ when he raised him from the dead and seated him at his right hand in the heavenly places, 21 far above all rule and authority and power and dominion, and above every name that is named, not only in this age but also in the one to come.

EPHESIANS 3 v 14-21

14 For this reason I bow my knees before the Father, 15 from whom every family in heaven and on earth is named, 16 that according to the riches of his glory he may grant you to be strengthened with power through his Spirit in your inner being, 17 so that Christ may dwell in your hearts through faith—that you, being rooted and grounded in love, 18 may have strength to comprehend with all the saints what is the breadth and length and height and depth, 19 and to know the love of Christ that surpasses knowledge, that you may be filled with all the fullness of God.

20 Now to him who is able to do far more abundantly than all that we ask or think, according to the power at work within us, 21 to him be glory in the church and in Christ Jesus throughout all generations, forever and ever. Amen.

PRAYER IS DEPENDENT

To pray is an admission and an expression of dependence.

A self-assured person is not going to pray prayers of petition; there's no need to pray if you think you have got it all covered. A self-righteous person is not going to pray prayers of confession; there's no need to pray if you think you're good enough to earn God's blessing. But the person who knows their heart before God—the person who knows the depth of their need of forgiveness and help from God—does what Paul does. They bow their knees (Ephesians 3 v 14).

Paul achieved great things. His ministry literally changed the world. His preaching set a fire raging round the Mediterranean—a gospel fire that stretched from Jerusalem up through Turkey into Greece and westwards to Rome. Few men have done as much, or had as great an impact, as this short, stooping, near-sighted Jewish convert.

But Paul never thought he did any of it alone. He knew he had a privileged task:

> *I was made a minister according to the gift of God's grace ... to preach to the Gentiles the unsearchable riches of Christ, and to bring to light for everyone what is the plan of the mystery hidden for ages in God, who created all things. (3 v 7, 8-9)*

And he knew that, without God's help, it would be an impossible task. So he prayed. He recognized the direct link between his preaching and his praying—the first must be accompanied by the second. He was aware of the fact that "unless the LORD builds the house, those who build it labor in vain" (Psalm 127 v 1). He lived out what the nineteenth-century hymnwriter Arthur C. Ainger described in "God Is Working His Purpose Out":

> *All we can do is nothing worth*
> *Unless God blesses the deed;*
> *Vainly we hope for the harvest-tide*
> *Till God gives life to the seed.*

This undergirds all of Paul's thinking. One plants the seed and another waters, but only God can make it grow (1 Corinthians 3 v 6-7).

THE PATTERN OF THE MASTER

In this, Paul was following the pattern of his Master, the Lord Jesus. As we read the Gospels, we discover that Jesus was praying to the Father all the time. Presumably, the many instances that the Gospel writers record for us were the tip of the iceberg, not the whole of it. Jesus' approach to life rested on dependent prayer. So the night before his death, in what we refer to as the upper room discourse, Jesus teaches his disciples in some of his most famous and moving words:

> *Let not your hearts be troubled. Believe in God; believe also in me. (John 14 v 1)*

> *I am the true vine ... As the Father has loved me, so have I loved you. Abide in my love. (15 v 1, 9)*

> *Greater love has no one than this, that someone lay down his life for his friends. (15 v 13)*

> *If the world hates you, know that it has hated me before it hated you. (15 v 18)*

> *When the Helper comes, whom I will send to you from the Father, the Spirit of truth, who proceeds from the Father, he will bear witness about me.*
> *(15 v 26)*

> *Take heart; I have overcome the world. (16 v 33)*

And then comes the first verse of chapter 17:

> *When Jesus had spoken these words, he lifted up his eyes to heaven, and said..."*

Jesus prayed. And he said, in effect, *Father, I'm praying now that the things that I have instructed my friends about, and that they have come to understand as a result of my teaching, may actually be their experience as they go out into the world.*

I find this a tremendous truth and a rather uncomfortable challenge. My prayers—whether I pray, how much I pray, about what I pray—reveal my priorities. And they reveal how much I really think I need God, or whether I am, deep down, in fact self-assured and self-righteous. If Paul, "an apostle of Christ Jesus by the will of God" (Ephesians 1 v 1), knew that he needed to "bow my knees before the Father" (3 v 14), what of us? If Jesus Christ, the greatest teacher in the world, followed up his instruction by prayer, what of us? If Jesus Christ, who was set on a mission that changed not just world history but all of eternity, took time to pray, what of us? If Jesus Christ, the Son of God, knew that he needed to pray, what of us?

MANNERS AT THE MEAL

This dependent prayer does not come naturally to us. If we think it will, then it will never happen.

Charles Simeon was minister of Holy Trinity in Cambridge, England, for a long time—54 years. In his congregation for some years was Henry Martyn, who would become an early missionary to India. On one occasion, having listened to Simeon preach, Martyn wrote in his diary:

> *Mr. Simeon, in his excellent sermon tonight, observed, that it was more easy for a minister to preach and study five hours, than to pray for his people for one half hour. (Journals and Letters of the Rev Henry Martyn, Vol. 1, page 171)*

It's true. Haven't you found that it is far easier to talk to others than to talk to God? Haven't you found it far easier to be engaged in busy activity, to be about good work, to be busy checking off the to-do list, than to stop and kneel before your Father? Aren't we usually on the wrong side of the Martha and Mary story? Aren't we more like Martha, who was so "distracted by much serving" that she did not join her sister Mary, who "sat at the Lord's feet and listened to his teaching," spending time with her Lord in conversation (Luke 10 v 39-40)?

Are you recognizing your dependence? That's the challenge. Remember, Paul knew the link between preaching and praying. So here is one way both to diagnose whether you are dependent and then to start to address any lack in your praying. Simply ask yourself: *will I pray before and after I hear God's word preached to me next Sunday?*

The way we come to listen to the Bible and the way we go off after we have listened—both on our own and also as a church—matters. And it is revealing. We tend to teach our children to say thank you to God for a meal before they eat it, and that you don't just walk away from the table after a meal; you say thank you before you get down. That's fair. It's just the same with the bread of God's word. You don't just start the meal—you thank God for it, and you ask him to use it to nourish you, spiritually. Then you don't finish the meal and run for your car; you finish the meal and you take some time to say, "Thank you, Father, for the food. It may not have been served the way I like it, it may not have been quite the flavor I was hoping for; but I believe the pastor, whoever he was, prayerfully prepared and delivered it as best as he could, and I want to thank you for providing for me before I head out."

HEART AND KNEES

So Paul writes this immense letter to the Ephesians, speaking of the glories and the wonders of God, and we look in on his bedroom (or rather, his prison), and where do we find him? On his knees, declaring his own helplessness. Even his posture is dependent. I think that's why he mentions it: "For this reason I bow my knees." Jewish men, by and large, prayed standing. Paul knelt, as an acknowledgment of who he was, and who the Father he was speaking to is. The great Victorian preacher C.H. Spurgeon said:

We may speak boldly with God, but still he is in heaven and we are upon earth, and are to avoid presumption.
(Lectures to My Students, Vol. 1, page 55)

We come confidently, but we do not come complacently. We come to a loving Father, but we do not come as his equal.

One day, at the name of Jesus every knee will bow as every tongue confesses that he truly is Lord, bringing glory to the Father (Philippians 2 v 10-11). As we look in upon Paul in his prison in Rome, he is getting a head start on things as he bows his knees. His posture is an expression both of the wonder and the awe that he feels before God and of his earnestness in seeking God. Paul's decision to pray is driven by his awareness of his dependence, and his posture in prayer emphasizes this awareness.

When you and I pray, that's really what we're saying. I'm not saying we must kneel. The posture of our hearts and not our bodies is the issue. Are we coming to God in dependence? Are we asking him to bless our work, to empower our service, to change our flaws, to forgive our sins? What matters is a dependent heart, not a particular posture, as one of my favorite poems makes hilariously clear:

"The proper way for a man to pray,"
Said Deacon Lemuel Keyes,
"And the only proper attitude,
Is down upon his knees."

"No, I should say the way to pray,"
Said Reverend Doctor Wise,
Is standing straight, with outstretched arms,
With rapt and upturned eyes."

"Oh no, no, no," said Elder Snow,
"Such posture is too proud:
A man should pray with eyes fast closed
And head contritely bowed."

"It seems to me one's hands should be
Astutely clasped in front,
With both thumbs pointed toward the ground,"
Said Reverend Doctor Blunt.

"Last year I fell in Hodgkin's well
Head first," said Cyrus Brown,
"With both my heels a-stickin' up,
And my head a-pointing down;
And I done prayed right there and then

Best prayer I ever said,
The prayingest prayer I ever prayed,
Standing on my head." (Sam Walter Foss)

The "prayingest prayer"—real prayer—is a prayer of a dependent person to a divine Person.

HE CAN FIX IT (YOU CAN'T)

This reminds us that there is, of course, such a thing as unchristian prayer. Looking within to find spiritual reality is not the same as praying to God. Self-help mantras are not the same as praying to the One who is our Helper. Equally, praying in some vague hope that the God who is up there, removed and distant, might care to hear and may just bother to act, is not the same as praying to a Father who we know loves us as he loves his Son.

Sometime last year when I picked up my mail, I discovered that the Church of Scientology had sent me a very nice magazine. Apparently, they're trying to recruit me. And I commend them for their attempt, though they will be disappointed with the results. But as I looked at the magazine, and I went to the back to see the aims of Scientology, I realized their view could be summed up in four words: *We can fix this.* Through our technology, through doing it our way, through our various stages of the "dianetic" discovery, you can be okay, they claim.

This is modern religion, and it comes in many guises (including a quasi-Christian one), but the view can always be summed up in those four words: *We can fix this.* So if you've got a problem, you need to know that it's not your fault. And if you're looking for an answer, look inside of you because you'll be able to fix it, or look to follow our rules or techniques because they'll be able to fix it. This view says, "Look into yourself, because you'll be able to find divinity in there if you search hard enough, and you'll sort yourself out if you find the right path and follow it well enough."

The Christian gospel says, "If you look into yourself, you will ultimately find only that which disappoints you and confronts you with your own ineptitude and your inability to fix even the simplest of the things that really matter. The problem is inside of you. It's your fault. And so the answer must come from outside of you and not rely upon you—so it is the most wonderful news that Jesus has come in order to fix your problem. He came to bring down the barrier between you and God, and restore you to the relationship you were made for, enjoying God as your loving Father."

It's the complete opposite.

This is why Christian prayer is uniquely dependent and humble; it's also reflective of the cry of every human heart. Even those who wouldn't name Jesus as their Lord and Savior, when they pause and are honest, acknowledge that something is broken and that they need help. Annie Lennox sums it up neatly in a song I keep on my phone (I'm a fan of Annie Lennox, only partly because she's Scottish). Called "Oh God," it asks God where he is and whether he is willing to help her, because she has "gone and broken everything." If ever there was a soul who needed saving, Annie sings, "it must be me … it must be now."

The Christian prays with more confidence than that song expresses—but with no less dependence. The more we realize our need, the more we will pray as Paul did; the more we will say, as he did, "I bow my knees before the Father." It's the heart attitude of dependence that counts, whether or not we express it physically by kneeling. But personally, I find it helpful to cause my body's posture to follow my heart posture. At our church, we kneel as elders as we pray in the prayer room before the services. We could sit; we could stand; we're free to do whatever we want, and our Father is not going to refuse us access to his heavenly throne room in prayer simply because our knees are not touching the floor. But we choose to kneel. It's an expression of our dependence upon God. It's good to do.

We will not pray big prayers if we do not pray at all. And if we are self-assured or self-righteous, our prayers at best will be irregular, impersonal, functional and prosaic. But Jesus was neither, and nor was Paul. Prayer reminds us who we are, and who our Father is. Prayer expresses our dependence and it reinforces our dependence.

For this reason, God's children bow their knee, in their hearts if not with their bodies, and they pray.

Father, thank you for the privilege of addressing you in this way. Help me to remember that the Lord Jesus obtained this access for me through his death on the cross. Please help me to remember that I am entirely dependent on the work of the Holy Spirit as I pray, and entirely dependent on you in my life in every way. Help me to learn to pray as I pray, for Jesus' sake. Amen.

PRADYER IS SPIRITUAL
(BUT NOT IMPRACTICAL)

When I read Paul's prayers, I am always struck by the fact that many of the matters that are the focus of my prayers are absent in his.

Read his prayers in his letter to the Ephesians (or anywhere else in his epistles), and what is striking is the absence of material issues. This absence is especially striking when we consider that Paul was in prison in Rome. But he doesn't pray about his predicament; he doesn't ask that he might be released. That would be legitimate—he's the one who wrote in Philippians 4 v 6…

> *Don't worry about anything; instead, pray about*
> *everything; tell God your needs, and don't forget to*
> *thank him for his answers.*
>
> *(Living Bible paraphrase)*

Paul wrote that, and he believed that, and so must we. But we also need to acknowledge with Paul the fact that these concerns are not the ultimate concerns. All that matters may be brought before God, but what we bring before God is not always what matters most.

SOMETHING BIGGER THAN HEALTH

The believers in Ephesus were in one sense just like us. They had concerns for food and for clothes and for shelter. They would have thought about and talked about and worried about being married or getting married… being parents or wishing they were parents, or wishing some days they weren't parents… employment, paying taxes, wealth, health… but there's no mention of these matters at all in what Paul prays for them.

In fact, praying about health (which, if we had the chance to listen in on the prayers of Western Christians, would likely come in at number one) is rare—almost non-existent—in the Bible. So why are we praying about it so much?

It's because we don't want to die.

We want to live. We've got a sneaking suspicion that what we've got now, this side of death, is actually better than what God has for us then, on the other side of death. So we want to hang on to what we've got. But instead, we need to believe—really believe—that these things are true:

> *God, being rich in mercy, because of the great love*
> *with which he loved us, even when we were dead in*
> *our trespasses, made us alive together with Christ—*
> *by grace you have been saved—and raised us up*
> *with him and seated us with him in the heavenly*

places in Christ Jesus, so that in the coming ages he might show the immeasurable riches of his grace in kindness toward us in Christ Jesus.

(Ephesians 2 v 4-7)

You have now been raised with Christ into the heavenly places. You have been made part of a family that will never come to an end. One day, you will live in a new heaven and a new earth. You will see your God face to face and, with a heart no longer burdened and distracted by sin and a body no longer broken and decaying in frailty, you will praise him.

And you and I just want to pray that we'd stay healthy and live long?! All that matters may be brought before God, but what we bring before God is not always what matters most.

When the eyes of our hearts are opened to our future, it changes our lives now—it reorders our priorities and our prayers. We pray less about the practical details of this life, and first and foremost about the spiritual realities of our eternal life. Eternal matters matter more; the concerns of today less. We live out, and we pray based on, the truth that "to live is Christ, and to die is gain" (Philippians 1 v 21).

But, time-bound and fallen creature that I naturally am, I often forget the spiritual and eternal element of reality. That's why the things that fill my prayers are so regularly absent from Paul's—and why the things that fill his prayers are so regularly absent from mine. He has his eyes fixed on eternity. His prayers are spiritual. We need to make ours so, too.

NO MORE "BE WITH"

To do that, I want to erase the two words that shut most of our prayers down. Here they are:

"Be with…"

If you were to record my prayers, I have a sad suspicion you'd hear a lot of "be with": "Dear Lord, I pray you will be with Tom as he goes to work, and be with Mary also, who's having her wisdom teeth removed on Tuesday, and be with… and be with… and be with… and be with us all. Amen."

This is unimaginative. It's limited. It's certainly not spiritually ambitious, like Paul is. And it is, I think, unnecessary. Jesus said, "Behold, I am with you always, to the end of the age" (Matthew 28 v 20). He's promised to be with Tom and with Mary. It's a bit of a waste to make the sum total of my prayer for them the request that Jesus would do what he already said he'd do, and has already started doing.

Search the Scriptures, and you won't find a prayer recorded that just asks God to "be with" his people. The prayers of the saints have far more weighty, far more spiritual concerns. Go to Nehemiah. In the opening section of Nehemiah, word comes to him in exile, working as the cupbearer of the Persian king, telling him that the walls of God's city, Jerusalem, are broken down and the gates are burned with fire. It is a complete fiasco up there. Nehemiah is brokenhearted by this; he decides that he will seek to do something about it. But, of course, he knows the truths we saw in the previous chapter of this book, and so…

As soon as I heard these words I sat down and wept and mourned for days, and I continued fasting and praying before the God of heaven. And I said..."
(Nehemiah 1 v 4-5)

You can read his prayer, right there in Nehemiah 1:

O LORD God, please be with all the people in Jerusalem...

No, he doesn't say that!

He says (and I'm paraphrasing), *O God, you great and awesome and magnificent God, who rules over the universe. We, your people, bow before you and confess our sins and our shortcomings before you.*

Can you see what he's doing? He's getting spiritual before he gets practical. He knows that the issue of the walls in Jerusalem is a metaphor for the real spiritual condition of the people. The reason that the wall is collapsed and broken down is because of the spiritual needs of their hearts. So Nehemiah prays first about what matters most: *Lord, I must confess our sins. Lord, I must acknowledge our complete dependence upon you. Lord, let us turn our gaze to the things that really matter, because we have completely lost sight of what's going on.*

Look at the prayers of Daniel, and he's the same. In Daniel 9, in the middle of the oppression of God's people, as chaos surrounds the people of God, he doesn't pray about practicalities. He prays about the grandeur and glory of God and his kingdom, and the fact that he is sovereign. It's immense. I'm humbled by him; I'm humbled by Nehemiah; I'm humbled by Paul. How small, how narrow-minded are my prayers. How "be with" are my prayers.

In my experience, those of us who are parents are particularly at risk of this kind of attitude when it comes to our children. If you have kids, here's one way to diagnose whether your prayers are over-practical and under-spiritual. What do you pray for your kids, when you pray for them (if you do)? Would our prayers for our children reveal that we understand that their spiritual condition matters more than their financial or relational or vocational well-being? Would our prayers reflect the truth that their position in Christ matters infinitely more than their position in school or college or the office or society?

All that matters may be brought before God, but we must always bring before God those things that matter most.

THE HUB

Don't take my word for this, though. Take Jesus' word.

In that famous passage in Matthew 6, Jesus talks to his followers about legitimate practical concerns—their food, their clothes, their lives. And he doesn't rebuke them for caring about those things. But he does say, *Let's think about this. Have you ever seen birds putting up a factory to make stuff? Why not? Because our Father feeds them. And have you ever seen the flowers sewing their clothes or heading down to the mall to make sure they have the right kit? Why not? Because no matter what clothes we manage to get, we'll never match the amazing natural beauty of God's creative handiwork. So,* Jesus says, *let me tell you what to do:*

*Seek first the kingdom of God and his
righteousness... (v 33)*

That's prioritizing spiritual things.

... and all these things will be added to you.

In other words, to paraphrase Jesus, he says, *If you take
care of my things, I'll take care of your things.*

The hub—the center of our lives and our actions—is
always spiritual. Think about a bicycle wheel—the hub
there is the key to all the spokes. If that hub is weak or
ill-fitting, so that the spokes are buckling, loose, or un-
attached, then the spokes will be ineffective and insuffi-
cient in enabling the wheel to take you in the direction
you need to go. The hub is crucial. And when it comes to
each of us, our hub is spiritual. The reason that Paul bows
his knees before the Father who is in heaven and prays in
this way is because he wants to show the Ephesians that
this is what really matters. And so spiritual matters are
what the focus of our prayers—not the entirety, but the
focus—must be.

SPIRITUAL CHANGE IS PRACTICALLY SEEN

When the spiritual hub of my life is solid, then the practical spokes will be strong. We tend to live as if, and pray
as if, what we most need is help with this practical issue
or that specific life problem. And we all have particular
situations that we need divine help with and divine transformation in. But it's as we grow in our appreciation of the
gospel that our lives will change to reflect that gospel.

The Ephesian Christians knew that because they'd experienced that. Ephesus was a city that was prosperous as a result of its ability to trade, and prominent on account of being the site of the great temple of Artemis or Diana, one of the seven wonders of the ancient world. That temple both drove pagan, magical worship and underpinned the local economy.

It was in that setting that Paul turned up and proclaimed the lordship of Jesus. Day after day, month after month, he "spoke boldly, reasoning and persuading them about the kingdom of God ... so that all the residents of Asia [modern-day Turkey] heard the word of the Lord, both Jews and Greeks" (Acts 19 v 8, 10).

Ephesus was a spiritual battleground. New believers were leaving a life dominated by the occult and by the power of spiritual forces (v 11-17). And that spiritual transformation led to practical change:

> *Many of those who were now believers came,*
> *confessing and divulging their practices. And a*
> *number of those who had practiced magic arts*
> *brought their books together and burned them in*
> *the sight of all. And they counted the value of them*
> *and found it came to fifty thousand pieces of silver.*
> *So the word of the Lord continued to increase and*
> *prevail mightily. (v 18-20)*

It must have been a quite magnificent bonfire as these Christians brought their books of magic together and burned them in a public forum. Don't miss the value of this reading material—fifty thousand pieces of silver.

That is a substantial amount of money. Imagine the conversations:

"What has happened to these people? Why are they burning all their books?"

"Well, they have a completely different view of the world."

"You mean they don't believe in spiritual stuff anymore?"

"Oh no, they do. But they've started to believe that Jesus of Nazareth is alive beyond his death, and that he forgives sins and that he is all-powerful over every sphere."

"Well, that sounds crazy. What idiots, to burn their books. They might at least have sold them."

The point is this: your hub—your spiritual belief system and view of God—drives your practical actions. And so when Paul wrote to the Ephesian church, he didn't say, *You need someone to sort out the political and civic structures of your city.* He didn't say, *You need to get some laws on the statute books that ban the riots you've been subjected to and the occult worship your city has been oppressed by.* No—Paul says to them, and us, that what we really need to know is the truth of the gospel. What we really need to know, or rather, who we really need to know, is Jesus. We need to know with assurance all that is ours in the Lord Jesus Christ. We need to know what is true of us now and we need to be aware of what will be true of us on the day when all things are wrapped up. Paul says, *I'm praying for that. You'll stand firm if you know truth.*

We're the same. What you and I need more than anything else is to be made experientially aware of the truth and reality of the Lord Jesus Christ—we need to know "the immeasurable greatness of his power toward us who believe" (Ephesians 1 v 19). Too often, our Jesus is too weak. We've got a view of Jesus that somehow puts him fighting for a place in the pantheon of gods—fighting for his position in the great story of spiritual history. We need to understand that Jesus wears a crown that infinitely outshines and eternally outlasts any and every other power—that he is, as the old hymn "Crown Him With Many Crowns" puts it, the Lord...

> *Whose power a scepter sways*
> *From pole to pole, that wars may cease,*
> *And all be prayer and praise.*

And we need to understand that he is...

> *... the Lord of years,*
> *The Potentate of time.*
> *Creator of the rolling spheres,*
> *Ineffably sublime. (Matthew Bridges)*

If we know this Jesus, we will each have a firm hub in the center of our lives, and we will each pray.

THOSE THINGS THAT MATTER MOST

So, when you start to pray, what's the concern that fills your vision?

You are facing a huge issue in your job? You need God's help with that, and so what you most need to know is the gospel. You need to know how to fix your marriage? You need God's help with that, and so what you most need to know is the gospel. You are so worried about something one of your kids is into? You need God's help with that, and so what you most need to know is the gospel. You are facing serious health problems? You need God's help with that, and so what you most need to know is the gospel.

We will see as we continue to enjoy Paul's prayers for the Ephesians how gospel truth makes a difference, in prayer and practicalities. But first, we need to start to pray spiritually. We need to start there—and then, as we move on to our practical concerns in our prayers, we need to let the way we pray about them flow from the spiritual truths we've prayed about. Let's not allow the focus of Paul's prayers to be absent from ours. All that matters may be brought before God, but we must always bring before God those things that matter most.

Father, thank you for not sparing your own Son and giving him up for us all. I know that this is what really matters. Thank you too that, along with him, you freely give us all things. For the many ways in which you provide for the practical concerns of my life, I praise you; and I ask that those practicalities would never become my sole or even primary focus. Help me to seek the help of the Holy Spirit in dealing with different and difficult matters, and most of all to remember what matters most. In Jesus' name. Amen.

PRAY FOR
FOCUS

We may be on our knees, dependently... we may be seeking to pray spiritually... but for most of us, sooner or later, the words don't come and the thought looms large: "OK, but *what do I say*?"

I want to pick out five great qualities for which Paul prays for his Ephesian brothers and sisters. We'll look at each in turn over the next five chapters. This is not an exhaustive list of what we may, can, and should pray for ourselves and our churches. But equally, you'll never exhaust the prayers on this list, even if you should pray them each day:

1. Pray for focus
2. Pray for hope
3. Pray for riches
4. Pray for power
5. Pray for love

FROM DARKNESS TO LIGHT

I once was lost but now I'm found,
Was blind, but now I see. ("Amazing Grace")

There is a very clear distinction between blindness and sight. You cannot be both blind and sighted simultaneously. That goes for the eyes of your heart as much as the eyes in your head.

I was blind, but now I see. That was, famously, the testimony of John Newton, the slave-trader turned pastor and hymnwriter. And that, of course, was also the testimony of Saul of Tarsus. When Saul met Jesus, Jesus caused his physical state to match the spiritual state with which he'd embarked on his journey to Damascus. He was struck blind. Then Ananias visited Saul, and…

> … *laying his hands on him he said, "Brother Saul,*
> *the Lord Jesus who appeared to you on the road by*
> *which you came has sent me so that you may regain*
> *your sight and be filled with the Holy Spirit." And*
> *immediately something like scales fell from his eyes,*
> *and he regained his sight. Then he rose and was*
> *baptized. (Acts 9 v 17-18)*

The scales falling from his eyes was emblematic of the spiritual transformation that Saul experienced as he realized, *So Jesus is alive. So Jesus is real. So Jesus is Lord.* He had been blind—so blind that he fought the light and arrested Jesus' followers. But now he saw—saw so clearly that he followed the Light of the world and proclaimed him throughout the known world.

And this metaphor runs through Paul's writings. Without spiritual sight, we'll see nothing that truly matters. And so he prays—not just for non-Christians, but for believers too:

> *... that the God of our Lord Jesus Christ, the Father of glory, may give you the Spirit of wisdom and of revelation in the knowledge of him, having the eyes of your hearts enlightened... (Ephesians 1 v 17-18)*

Your heart is the very center of your existence—your core. It's the headquarters of who and what you are—your mind, your emotion, your will. And you need the eyes of that heart opened wide and focused well.

LEARNING TO SEE

When a baby is born, he or she can see a bit. But they can only see in black and white, and they see everything upside down, until the brain works out (I have no idea how) that things would make more sense the other way up. When you are born again, you stop being blind and you see. But the eyes of your heart take time to get used to the light, to focus. You see quite a bit, but you don't see everything. And so Paul is praying here that those who have come to faith in Jesus may have the eyes of their hearts enlightened, so that they might see clearly.

What is it he wants them to see? Well, he has just spent eleven verses—and, in the Greek, it is a single, long, joyful sentence—giving us his great symphony of salvation, a great hymn of praise. He's been assuring his readers of all that is theirs in the Lord Jesus Christ:

- They are chosen to be holy and blameless in God's sight (v 4).
- They were predestined to be God's adopted children, loved as his eternal Son is loved (v 5).
- They are redeemed by the blood of Jesus, so that they can enjoy the reality of knowing that although they are sinners, they are *forgiven* sinners (v 7).
- They have been brought into the great plan of the Father to bring all things into unity and perfection under the glorious rule of his Son (v 9-10).
- They have an inheritance of eternity with him ahead of them, and the Spirit from him dwelling in them, guaranteeing that they will reach that place (v 11, 13-14).

Don't take this for granted. We should be surprised to be part of God's people. After all, he did not choose us because of anything we brought to his team. All you and I brought were our transgressions. Even the faith we placed in Christ to forgive us was a gift from him (Ephesians 2 v 8-9).

In my church, we sometimes sing a hymn—"The Family of God" by Gloria and William J. Gaither—that contains the line, "I'm so glad I'm a part of the family of God." Being more honest, we should sing, "I'm surprised that I'm part of the family of God," because it *is* quite surprising that God would choose you, and me. You should be amazed that the love of God for you goes back into eternity. That before he created the world he set his love upon you. That at a particular moment in the history of the world, he drew you to himself. That despite your complexities and your flaws and your failings, he loves you. You don't deserve that. It's by faith, which is a gift of God. Paul was unceasingly thankful for what God had done for the Ephesian Christians (v 16)—he purposefully remembered them in his prayers, giving thanks for their faith. And we must be thankful too, for ourselves and for those we know who have faith—for truly, God has blessed his people "with every spiritual blessing in the heavenly places" (v 3).

The problem is that so often we don't see it.

And so in verse 15 Paul moves from praise to prayer—and in verses 16-17 he prays that these Christians might really see what they have. He's gone through this amazing though not exhaustive list of things God has provided for them. And he says, *Now do you really see this? If you really understood this, then it would revolutionize your life.* And the answer he's expecting is, *No, I don't, not all the time. Sometimes I don't see this at all, really.* So he says, *I'm praying for you, that the eyes of your hearts may be opened.*

There was an English preacher called S.D. Gordon who would ask his congregation, "Are you listening with all the ears of your heart?" And Paul is saying, *You need to look with both the eyes of your heart. You need to see all that is really true of you, in Christ.*

Paul's praying not for new sight but for focused sight. He's praying not for his readers to become Christians but to enjoy all that is theirs as Christians. He knows about their "faith in the Lord Jesus" and their "love toward all the saints" (v 15). He's giving thanks that God has opened their eyes to see who Jesus is. But Paul's not settling for that. He wants more for them. Faith in Christ is first of all a decisive act, and then it is a sustained attitude. It is to have your heart-eyes opened to who Jesus is and what he has done; and then it is to have your heart-eyes more and more focused on the glory of Jesus, so you live more and more in light of that. Paul wants the Ephesians to understand and enter into the benefits they have already received.

Too often, as Christians we live like someone who has been given a full-board ticket on a cruise ship, and who sits on their deckchair eating crackers and drinking water because they haven't realized that all the food is free with their ticket. They never go to the restaurant because they haven't understood just what it is that their ticket includes. They're on the boat—but they're not enjoying being on the boat.

Paul says to the Ephesian Christians, *You need to know, you need to see, that you have been given "every spiritual blessing." Not one. Not some. Every one.* That's what transforms you, both inside and outside. So Paul says, *It is my prayer that the eyes of your hearts will be illuminated, so that you might know what you are looking at.*

And supremely, you are looking at Christ.

YOU NEED TO KNOW GOD

It is in Jesus that all our spiritual blessings are given. It is in the Son that the Father has made himself known. The more clearly you see Christ, the more wonderful he will seem to you and the more gloriously your life in him will be revealed to you. That's what Paul wants his friends to see—he wants "the God of our Lord Jesus Christ, the Father of glory [to] give you the spirit of wisdom and revelation *in the knowledge of him*" (v 17, my italics). You need God to do this for you. It is the work of God the Father Almighty, through the work of the Spirit of God, to bring home the benefits that he has made available to us through the Son of God, so that the people of God might become all that he desires for them to be.

We need to learn to pray, "Open the eyes of my heart, Lord. I want to see you, and all I have in you." Knowing God by seeing God. This is what we most need. One of the major weaknesses of evangelicalism today is a failure at this very level. Wherever I preach, I often find people saying afterwards, "But you haven't told me what to *do*. Can you give me something practical? Something that I can *do* that will help me?"

Part of the answer lies in this prayer of Paul's. Nowhere in any of Paul's letters will you find a six-step guide to satisfaction, or the four keys to anxiety-free living, or eight practical ways to make the most of your money. No—Paul wants for you what you most need. *What you really need,* he says, *is a spirit of wisdom and revelation, that leads to a greater, deeper knowledge of him.* You need to know God.

This is a lonely world. We so often feel ourselves alone. Social media isn't satisfying (however many likes you get). Friends let us down or are busy. Everybody wants somebody to come and help, to come and hold their hand. Let me tell you what you need. You need to look at God. You need to know God. You need to know there is a Creator and a Sustainer of everyone and everything, and that he is your kind Father. You need to know that he is slow to chide and he's swift to bless. You need to know that he understands your needs and that he answers your prayers. You need to know that he chose you, he adopted you, he secured your destiny, he forgave you, and he sent his Spirit to you. Why? Because he loves you. You need to see all that you have in Christ, in glorious full-color focus.

God has "blessed us in Christ with every spiritual blessing in the heavenly places" (v 3). Can you see it? Can you see him?

This is what will change you, reassure you, and ground you. The most transformational thing you can do today is to look clearly at Christ with the eyes of your heart. "We all, with unveiled face, beholding the glory of the Lord, are being transformed into the same image from one degree of glory to another" (2 Corinthians 3 v 18). How do you do that? You can't do it yourself. The blind man does not cure himself. "This comes from the Lord who is the Spirit" (v 18). Which means it is possible to pray for it, and necessary to pray for it, and infinitely worth praying for it. Pray that "the eyes of your heart may be enlightened" (Ephesians 1 v 18, NIV), so that you could truly say of yourself, "I was blind to him, but now I see him—more and more and more!"

Gracious God, thank you for opening the eyes of my heart, enabling me to see that in Christ you have given me "every spiritual blessing in the heavenly places." Forgive me for the times when I allow other things to cloud my vision. Help me to live looking to Jesus, so that I can learn to view everything in light of this reality—that from you and through you and to you are all things. For Jesus' sake. Amen.

PRAY FOR HOPE

Most of the ways we use the word, "hope" is all about uncertainty. "I hope I don't trip." "I hope it doesn't rain tomorrow." "I hope the stock market rectifies itself." It's got no sense of confidence.

But the New Testament, when it uses the word "hope," knows nothing of uncertainty. God wants us to "know what is the hope to which he has called you" (Ephesians 1 v 18). To know this hope is to know the assurance of a reality that you have not yet fully experienced. It is not something that is in doubt. It is something that has been promised by the God of truth. It is a secure hope. It is a hope that breeds confidence. It is a hope based on the knowledge that "those whom he foreknew he also predestined to be conformed to the image of his Son" (Romans 8 v 29), and "he who began a good work in you will bring it to completion" (Philippians 1 v 6).

So, Paul says to the Ephesian Christians, *I am praying that you might actually know the hope to which God has called you in Christ Jesus.* He doesn't simply mean only an intellectual knowledge; he means knowing both intellectually and experientially. Hope is objective—it is a reality based on truth. And hope is subjective—the reality is something I take hold of with my heart. Biblical hope is what enables our hearts to remain calm when we think, "I'm going to die one day." Biblical hope means our hearts respond to the thoughts of our own death by saying, "Jesus is risen. My faith is there, in him. He's my hope. He won't fail me."

NO AND KNOW

I see this come across at funerals of believers very clearly. Funerals are moments where people come face to face with mortality—face to face with hope or hopelessness. And in the words of committal, we say:

> *For as much as it has pleased Almighty God in*
> *his great mercy to receive unto himself the soul of*
> *our dear brother/sister here departed, we therefore*
> *commit his/her body to the ground. Ashes to ashes,*
> *and dust to dust, in the sure and certain hope of*
> *eternal life through our Lord Jesus Christ.*

I often get adults—and children—asking me afterwards, "How can that work? How can you have a sure hope, a certain hope?" If it's hope, it can't be sure and certain; and if it's sure and certain, it's not hope. And so I explain how the hope God gives is different—that here we are referring to a reality that is absolutely assured but that is not yet fully experienced.

It is on the strength of that hope that we approach our own demise. And it is the absence of that hope which pervades secular funerals throughout the Western world.

Joe Queenan, who writes for *The Wall Street Journal* every so often, has written a number of books. He's funny and clever, and not a little cynical. In one of his books, *Balsamic Dreams*, he writes a chapter about the Baby Boomer generation, of which he is a part, and the way that he thinks they have attempted to cover up and to deny the pervasive sense of hopelessness which is part and parcel of the average funeral. He says that, unable to face the reality of our mortality, we turn it into a party. We turn it into a video show. We turn it into whatever we can turn it into to try and deny the reality of death itself. Why is that? Because death is hopeless. It saps the hope from life because it promises the end of everything. No achievement or accumulation can survive the finality of death. As Paul puts it in Ephesians 2, without the gospel we were without hope and without God in the world (v 12). We were "dead in … trespasses and sins … by nature children of wrath, like the rest of mankind" (v 1-3). No God, no hope.

"But God…"—what glorious words!—"being rich in mercy, because of the great love with which he loved us, even when we were dead in our trespasses, made us alive together with Christ" (v 4-5).

Know God, know hope.

The hope of the gospel is real. It is certain. And it needs to be embraced emotionally as well as understood intellectually. So the question is: Do you have this hope? Have the blessings that God has provided in Jesus laid hold upon your heart and mind in such a way that they have become personal to you? Is it true of you that in every realistic sense your entire confidence both in life and in death is grounded in the person and work of the Lord Jesus Christ?

Do you know that hope?

And if not, then what is your plan?

YOU ARE GOING TO LIVE FOREVER

It's worth being straightforward for a moment, because the West is full of people who call themselves Christians but who don't know anything of this hope, and are instead indulging the uncertain hope that when it comes to it, there'll be some kind of automatic pass to heaven, or some amount of goodness will see them through. Some of those people will probably read this book.

So ask yourself, "What is my hope when I consider the fact of my own death?"

We don't talk much about our deaths in churches, let alone in our culture, but experience tells us that one out of one dies, and the Bible says that when we die, we will meet God. We've got an appointment with our Maker. Whether you die as a believer or as an unbeliever, you're going to be raised from the dead, forever. You will spend eternity either in the perfect, loving, blessing presence of God, which the Bible calls heaven, or absent the perfect, loving, blessing presence of God, which the Bible calls hell.

The story of the Bible is the story of a God who seeks out people who are hiding from him. He's been doing that since the first humans rebelled against him and hid in the garden he'd made for them to enjoy with him. God didn't say to Adam and Eve, *Well, OK—you go ahead and do what you want.* No, he came. He spoke. He called out to Adam.

And he comes still today, to those who are hiding from him. And he says, *Why are you hiding? Don't you know that I've provided forgiveness and all you need in Jesus? Don't you know that I have loved you to such an extent that I sent my Son to take your place and your judgment so that you need never fear judgment on that future day. Don't you know that I have made this available to you? Why would you hide from all that?*

And people say, "Well, I guess so. It kind of makes sense. But it's not for me," Or, "My wife, she's into this whole thing—but not me." Or, "That stuff, it's for kids, or folks who have time on their hands, or who have messed up. I'm doing OK as I am, thanks."

But what's the plan? If the hope is not Jesus, what's the plan for that day, whose date is fixed, when you have an appointment with God, whose verdict is final and eternal? If the love of God won't draw you off the fence, then let the fear of death and beyond scare you off it.

God is seeking people, asking people, to come into a real, living, hope-filled relationship with him. He comes to find lost sinners. Maybe it's someone knocking on the door. Maybe it's something a grandchild says. Maybe it's a friend with a book. Maybe it's someone's life unraveling and them testifying to how Jesus was real and trustworthy and loving all the way through it. However it is that God is coming to you, you need to take hold of the hope he is holding out. You need to ask God to open your heart-eyes to it. You are going to live forever. The only question is where.

HE WENT TO PREPARE A PLACE

In John 14, the night before his death, Jesus is comforting his disciples, and he makes this glorious promise:

> *Let not your hearts be troubled. Believe in God;*
> *believe also in me. In my Father's house are many*
> *rooms. If it were not so, would I have told you that I*
> *go to prepare a place for you? And if I go and prepare*
> *a place for you, I will come again and will take you*
> *to myself, that where I am you may be also. (v 1-3)*

Read these words, and know that, if you have placed your trust in Jesus, who conquered death and walked out the other side of it, he is saying them to you: *I went to prepare a place for you. I will come again and take you to myself, that where I am you may be also.*

Drink it in. Let your heart, as well as your head, know this: *I went to prepare a place for you. I will come again and take you to myself, that where I am you may be also.*

I remember back when I was a boy in Scotland, the winters were freezing. Sometimes I would go out, and my father would tell me to be home by a certain time. And when I arrived back home, I would find that my father had made my bed up for me. He'd put a hot water bottle in my bed. He was ready to welcome me. I can still remember the thrill of knowing in that moment that I had a father who loved me. He'd prepared all that for me. *Yes, son, I was looking forward to you coming. I knew you would be home soon. I got your room ready for you.*

This is the hope to which Jesus has called you. This is the hope Jesus came to give you. The life of Jesus, the death of Jesus, the resurrection of Jesus, the ascension of Jesus—each says to us, *I've got your room ready for you.*

In this certain hope lies the Christian's hope and confidence and excitement. We know our best days are all ahead of us. We know that death isn't the end of the best time of our life; it's the start of it.

That's hard to remember. That's hard to cling onto in a world that's hopeless and in circumstances that can sometimes look hopeless. And that's hard to wrap our heads around—eternity is too vast for our minds to cope with. But we can look at Jesus, and let our confidence grow. When the great English pastor John Stott was once asked a question about the nature of life after death, he quoted this verse that the seventeenth-century Puritan pastor Richard Baxter had penned:

> *My knowledge of that life is small.*
> *The eye of faith is dim.*
> *But 'tis enough that Christ knows all,*
> *And I shall be with him.*
> ("Lord, It Belongs Not To My Care")

Christ has gone ahead, and Christ has prepared your place. It's hard to see day by day. Even when we understand intellectually, we may give in to fear emotionally. That's why you need to ask God to make your hope real to you, and ask God to make it real to those around you. Pray for a focus on your hope. A great prayer for yourself each day, and for Christian friends on their darker days, is simply this:

Heavenly Father, I confess that I am often fearful and tempted to look for fulfillment and security in things that promise but do not deliver. Help me to deal with experiences of disappointment, defeat and sadness as one who has been reborn to a living hope by the resurrection of the Lord Jesus. Thank you that this sure and certain hope stands the test of time and strengthens me as each day demands. Lord, let me see the certainty and the glory of the hope to which you've called me. Let calm and confidence flow from that, Lord. For Jesus' sake. Amen.

PRAY FOR RICHES

One day, you and I are going to be very, very rich.

That's because we have an inheritance ahead of us. In Ephesians 1 v 14, Paul says the Holy Spirit dwelling in God's people is "the guarantee of our inheritance until we acquire possession of it." Our inheritance is already ours, but we have not taken ownership of it all. There is more that yet awaits us, and we'll enjoy it when we enter into glory. For you to benefit from an inheritance, a death is required. Usually, it's someone else's death. Here, it's yours.

And so Paul prays that you and I will know what we will one day own and experience: that the eyes of our hearts would be enlightened to "know ... what are the riches of his glorious inheritance in the saints" (v 18).

This kind of prayer was clearly a habitual one for Paul. He prayed in similar manner for the church in Colossae to "be strengthened with all power, according to [God's] glorious might, for all endurance and patience with joy, giving thanks to the Father, who has qualified you to share in the inheritance of the saints in light" (Colossians 1 v 11-12). And this emphasis is not merely found in Paul's epistles but throughout the Bible. Peter encourages his readers along the same lines:

> *[God] has caused us to be born again to a living hope through the resurrection of Jesus Christ from the dead, to an inheritance that is imperishable, undefiled, and unfading, kept in heaven for you, who by God's power are being guarded through faith for a salvation ready to be revealed in the last time. (1 Peter 1 v 3-5)*

Your inheritance is unfading, Peter says. It's never going to dissipate or disappoint. It will be there exactly as God has planned, ready to be entered into on the day when God, who is shielding you on your journey, gets you to that destination.

WE GET GOD

What is so good about this inheritance? Why is it so wonderful that it can bring us joy and perseverance on the journey towards it, though "you have been grieved by various trials" (v 6)?

The answer is that the inheritance is so glorious, the riches are so glittering, because the inheritance is God: God himself. The riches we stand to inherit are what Paul calls in Ephesians 3 v 16 "the riches of his glory."

What is the glory of God? The glory of God is the summation of his being. The glory of God is the sum and substance of all that he has revealed to us of himself, which our limited minds are able to glimpse and that our perfected minds will one day grasp.

So, for example, God's glory is his might, his self-existence, his majesty, his justice, his truth, his righteousness, his holiness, his purity… we could go on. It is the perfection that we see manifested in the human character of Jesus—the Word, who, John says, became flesh and dwelt among us so that we might say, "We have seen his glory, glory as of the only Son from the Father, full of grace and truth" (John 1 v 14).

And one day, you are going to see that glory face to face, and you are going to enjoy it as you praise him for eternity.

I don't know if there's ever been someone for you with whom you just wanted to spend all your time. You couldn't conceive of growing bored of their company, and when they weren't with you, everything was a little less colorful because of their absence. Well, God is infinitely perfect. There is always more of him and more about him to appreciate and to enjoy, and so his company is unimaginably perfect.

And he is your inheritance.

The greatest gift of God to his people is God. The greatest joy of heaven is God.

That's your inheritance, which you're walking towards today. Paul prays that we would know it and enjoy the prospect of it.

Now again, it's easy to think, "Well, this seems a bit remote from life. I was hoping this book would be a little more practical than this."

Ah, but to speak about the riches of the glory of God the Father, the Son and the Spirit—of his unsurpassable majesty and magnificence, of his grace and his truth—is actually of fundamental importance to your life, to your job, to your relationships, to your everything. As the young C.H. Spurgeon preached it to his congregation in London in 1855:

> *Would you lose your sorrows? Would you drown your cares? Then go, plunge yourself in the Godhead's deepest sea; be lost in his immensity; and you shall come forth as from a couch of rest, refreshed and invigorated. I know nothing which can so comfort the soul; so calm the swelling billows of grief and sorrow; so speak peace to the winds of trial, as a devout musing upon the subject of the Godhead.*
> *(The New Park Street Pulpit, Vol. 1, Sermon No. 1)*

This is where we must start. You can have as many how-to books as you want. You can try as many practical solutions as you can find. But to start there is to start from the wrong end.

It is to God, into the vast reservoir of the riches of his glory, that we go first, and out of the abundance of his provision and in anticipation of one day living in his full, unshielded glory, the other things fall into line.

I'm praying that you would be animated and excited each day by the prospect of your glorious inheritance, says Paul.

But that's not all. Our inheritance is God. And God's inheritance is... us.

GOD GETS...

The Bible commentators are divided over the nature of the "inheritance" in Ephesians 1 v 18. You can read it as regarding the inheritance with is ours—God. And you can also read it as speaking of the inheritance which God has prepared for himself—us. In other words, we can see Paul as speaking about "his [God's] ... inheritance in the saints". The notions are two sides of one coin. They're not mutually exclusive. God has an inheritance in his people and we have an inheritance in Christ.

Looking at this side of the coin, then, Paul is referring to the fact that the Father has promised the Son an inheritance—and that inheritance is made up of all who are in Christ.

The prophet Malachi spoke of it in this way:

> *Then those who feared the LORD spoke with one*
> *another. The LORD paid attention and heard them,*
> *and a book of remembrance was written before*
> *him of those who feared the LORD and esteemed his*
> *name. "They shall be mine, says the LORD of hosts,*
> *in the day when I make up my treasured possession,*
> *and I will spare them as a man spares his son who*
> *serves him." (Malachi 3 v 16-17)*

And the psalmist, as he called God's people to "Shout for joy in the LORD" for "praise befits the upright," declared:

> *Blessed is the nation whose God is the LORD, the*
> *people whom he has chosen as his heritage!*
> > *(Psalm 33 v 1, 12)*

There you have this Old Testament picture of God seeing in his people an inheritance that is his.

I remember in Sunday school as a child enjoying singing a song called "When He Cometh," written by an American man named W.O. Cushing. It's arguably a sentimental song, but I loved it as a boy, and I still love it as a man:

> *When He cometh, when He cometh,*
> *To make up His jewels,*
> *All His jewels, precious jewels,*
> *His loved and His own,*
> *He will gather, He will gather*
> *The gems for His kingdom,*
> *All the pure ones, all the bright ones,*
> *His loved and His own.*
> *Little children, little children,*
> *Who love their Redeemer,*
> *Are the jewels, precious jewels,*
> *His loved and His own.*
> *Like the stars of the morning,*
> *His bright crown adorning,*
> *They shall shine in their beauty,*
> *Bright gems for His crown.*

Arguably sentimental—but nevertheless truthful. What a wonderful picture. We get to inherit God—which is awesome; and God gets to inherit us—which, to be honest, is strange. God has chosen to spend eternity with… you! And me! He has purposed to enjoy spending his time, for all of time, with a multitude of redeemed, forgiven, ex-sinful humans.

Believer, God is very excited about seeing you. You will not sneak into heaven through the back door, quietly, and have God tolerate you for eternity. You will be welcomed in through the front door, with a party, and have God enjoy you as you enjoy him for eternity. God will enjoy being surrounded by human-shaped trophies of his grace. And you will enjoy his welcome and his embrace.

LOOKING BEYOND THE HORIZON OF NOW

Paul is praying that we will "know" this. We need to pray this for ourselves and others. We need to look up from our present problems, mistakes, regrets, and sadnesses and look forward to that future inheritance. We will need God's help to do that—to get our heart-eyes open and focusing on our future. Naturally, we live with a horizon of now. We look no further than our eyelids. And often today is dark. And sometimes today has those bits of light in it, the good things in our lives, but they change and they can disappear, and if that's all we look at, then hope is fleeting and joy proves elusive. So Paul teaches you to ask God to open your heart-eyes to see much further and see much better, to the riches of your eternity.

There can be joy even in the hardest times and hope even in the darkest hours if your eyes are looking to your future. Will you ask the Lord not just to get you through life but to open your heart-eyes to look at your inheritance with God? Will you ask the Lord to do that for Christians you know who are struggling in this life? And will you ask the Lord to do that for Christians you know who are succeeding in this life? Ask God to make your vision, and their vision, himself—to say and sing and mean the great truth that…

Riches I heed not, nor man's empty praise;
Thou mine inheritance, now and always.
                    (Eleanor Hull, "Be Thou My Vision")

We are richer than we realize. And one day in glory, we will be richer than we can even begin to imagine. We'll be with God.

Father, may my praying always show me to be one of your children. You are a generous God, giving me abundant blessings. Thank you that your supreme gift is the gift of yourself. Yet how easily and quickly I forget you, and focus instead on earthly, flimsy treasure. Your word tells me that if I know how to give good gifts to my children, then how much more will you give your children all that we need and far more than we deserve. Thank you that the cross proves the truth of this to me. Please help me to live out that truth today. In Christ's name I earnestly pray. Amen.

PRAY FOR POWER

Not many of us feel powerful. In fact, we often feel ourselves to be the antithesis of powerful—we feel ourselves to be weak. We know what it is to be tempted and to succumb and to fail. We know what it is to be tried and to be tested. We know what it is to be overwhelmed: to wake up in the morning and feel overwhelmed by uncertainty; to wake at three o'clock in the morning almost overwhelmed by anxieties. We know what it is to experience fears about our future, regrets about our past, worries about our health, and concerns about our loved ones.

None of us are immune to any of this. Neither were the Ephesians. And neither was Paul—he told the church in Corinth that on his first visit to that city, "I was with you in weakness and in fear and much trembling" (1 Corinthians 2 v 3). *And so,* says Paul to the church in Ephesus, *I'm praying that you might know "the immeasurable greatness of his power toward us who believe"* (Ephesians 1 v 19). He's praying for power.

What kind of power is this, which is available to us who believe? Paul takes us to three places. Number one is the resurrection: the "working of his great might that he worked in Christ when he raised him from the dead" (v 19-20). Number two is the exaltation of Jesus: God "seated him at his right hand in the heavenly places." Number three is the dominion of Jesus: he is "far above all rule and authority and power and dominion, and above every name that is named, not only in this age but also in the one to come. And he put all things under his feet" (v 21). Paul says that you and I need to have an understanding of the comprehensive nature of the triumphant victory of Jesus, and that the power that accomplished that victory is the power that is available to you and me—powerless, frail clay pots that we naturally are.

POWER THAT RAISES THE DEAD

At the very heart of our Christian testimony is the resurrection of the Lord Jesus: a resurrection which was testified to by a tomb that was empty, and that could not be (and never has been) explained away. The fact of the matter is that the only reasonable explanation is that it happened just as Jesus said it would happen.

The transformation of the disciples is a testimony again to the reality of the resurrection. They had been defeated. They had given up. They had hidden away. The body of Jesus was buried in the tomb of Joseph of Arimathea, and there was nothing left to say or do. And then suddenly they were out on the street, and Peter was saying, "This Jesus God raised up, and of that we all are witnesses ... Know for certain that God has made him both Lord and

Christ, this Jesus whom you crucified" (Acts 2 v 32, 36). Where did you get this power from, Peter? You were a bewildered man—a defeated man, a denier. Before all that, you were just a fisherman. How come you're back? How come you're bold? It's the work of the immeasurable greatness of God's power—the same power that raised Peter's Lord from the dead raised Peter and the rest of those disciples from the doldrums of their own uncertainty and lack of faith.

Absent the reality of the resurrection, we would not have a page of the New Testament. The apostles would have had no gospel to preach, and we would have no story to tell. But the fact is, as Luke tells us in Acts, that the Father made sure that his Holy One did not see corruption (Acts 2 v 30-31). The body of Jesus did not disintegrate in the tomb of Joseph of Arimathea. Not for a moment. Why? Because of the immeasurable greatness of God's power in accomplishing this physical, objective, historical resurrection of a man from death.

JESUS IS NOT ONLY RISEN

But the resurrection does not stand alone. Jesus has not only been resurrected but he has been exalted to the right hand of the Father in the heavenly places. He has now returned to the place from which he had come.

The Bible writers see the resurrection and the ascension as just one movement. Jesus is both the risen Lord and the ascended King. The ascension is a display of his amazing power just as much as the resurrection. The ascension completed the work of Christ by proving the full acceptance of the Father for Christ's one sacrifice for sin. In the ascension, as the writer of the book of Hebrews puts it, "when Christ had offered for all time a single sacrifice for sins, he sat down at the right hand of God" (Hebrews 10 v 12). Where is Jesus, right at this moment, as you read this? He is sitting down, at the right hand of God, his sacrifice for sins lying in the past, his preparing of a place in glory for his people lying in the past, his sending of his Spirit to gift and empower the church lying in the past.

WHAT JESUS IS DOING NOW

So what is Jesus doing now? He is governing the universe. In his power, the Father has "put all things under his feet and [given] him as head over all things" (Ephesians 1 v 22). This is what theologians call the session of Christ (from the Latin verb meaning "to sit," from which we get the phrase "the court is now in session"—the judge is seated to exercise his jurisdiction). Jesus is seated at the right hand of the Father not to rest but to rule. He is upholding the universe (Hebrews 1 v 3), and he is directing the universe. To what end? God "gave him as head over all things to the church" (Ephesians 1 v 22). As he governs all things, he works in all things for the good of those who love him, his church. As the theologian Herman Hoeksema explained:

> *The relationship between Christ's power over all things and his sovereignty over the church is such that he employs the former to the preservation and salvation of the latter.*
>
> *("The Doctrine of the Church" in*
> *The Standard Bearer, Vol. 40, Issue 2)*

So when we approach the heavenly throne in prayer, embarrassed by our sin, bedraggled by our burdens, weakened in our inadequacies, we discover it to be a throne of grace. We approach it in the awareness of the fact that the One who upholds the universe and governs his church helps its members.

THAT POWER, IN YOU

What would be the effect of knowing "the immeasurable greatness of his power toward us who believe"? It would be that we would live lives of wholehearted action. When we get this in perspective, it changes everything in our view of the world. The immeasurable greatness of his power galvanizes us. Why? Because there is no reason why we cannot obey God; there is no reason why we cannot witness to God. Jesus told his first disciples after his resurrection and before his ascension:

> *Thus it is written, that the Christ should suffer and on the third day rise from the dead, and that repentance for the forgiveness of sins should be proclaimed in his name to all nations, beginning from Jerusalem. You are witnesses of these things. And behold, I am sending the promise of my Father upon you. But stay in the city until you are clothed with power from on high. (Luke 24 v 46-49)*

> *You will receive power when the Holy Spirit has come upon you, and you will be my witnesses in Jerusalem and in Judea and Samaria, and to the end of the earth. (Acts 1 v 8)*

The fact of the matter is that without the power that comes from God's Spirit, the disciples could do nothing. With that power, they could do anything in the cause of God's Son. This was the power that raised Christ from the dead, and it was the power that drove the mission of the church out from Jerusalem and throughout the Roman world within one generation. That is the power that is available to you and me. That is the power that can energize our wholehearted action, which can see us stand up and speak up for Christ. Paul prayed that his Ephesian friends would know that power, and live as though that power were real because they knew the resurrection was real. Will you pray the same for yourself?

When I look at myself, I see my powerlessness, and it holds me back. I think about myself. How's it going for me? Am I doing well? Can I manage this? Is this too much of a risk? I need to look at Christ—not see him as a Galilean peasant wandering around, but see him as the ascended King, seated in a position of authority above all rule and authority and power and dominion, and above every name that has been named. That's what I need.

It is the supremacy of Christ which is the basis of safety and security for the Christian. Do you know anyone else who can forgive your sins? No, but you do not need to. Do you know of anyone else in the universe who has conquered death and opened up the way for you to pass through death? No, but you do not need to. Do you know anyone else who is directing things for your good—who knows the worst of you and loves you nevertheless, enough to be always working for your good? No, but you do not need to.

Christ's position and presence and power are the anti-dote to our fears. When I'm aware of fears without, when I'm conscious of my weakness within, when I'm aware of the fact that I am not all that I should be, I can rest in the fact of his authority and in his power.

"OK," we say: "All this power that my Savior has and makes available to me through his Spirit—but I lost my job. All this power—and my health is failing. All this power—and my spouse has died. All this power—and sin still persists. All this power—and I feel so weak."

Well, this is not heaven yet. Experiencing the immea-surable greatness of God's power does not mean we do not cry, we do not mourn, we do not question. But as we do all that, we must still bow. And we can still walk forwards. We may not understand what he is doing right now, but we bow beneath his rule and his authority, and we trust his power will lead us through and enable us to obey. Along that path there is safety. And if you talk to Christians who have lived for long enough to have expe-rienced the ups and downs and the failures and the foi-bles and the mess, then most of them will tell you that the greatest progress that they've made in the journey of faith has not been in triumph but in affliction. We expe-rience the power of God keeping us going and keeping us growing, keeping us obeying and keeping us witnessing, not when the band is playing and everybody's marching, but when the music has faded and we are crawling along.

When you come to the end of your power, that is where you find his. And when you do, you'll find that it is im-measurable and therefore that it is enough:

In heavenly love abiding,
No change my heart shall fear;
And safe is such confiding,
For nothing changes here:
The storm may roar about me,
My heart may low be laid;
But God is round about me,
And can I be dismayed?
(Anna Laetitia Waring, "In Heavenly Love Abiding")

Not many of us feel powerful. Indeed, we are not. But we have a power that comes from beyond our fallen minds and frail bodies. Live with a sight of the risen, ascended, reigning Christ, and know that the power that set him there is yours today. Don't let anybody—including yourself—tell you differently. Rest in his promises. Live in his presence. Pray that you would not just know about, but know the lived reality of, "the immeasurable greatness of his power toward us who believe." And by God's grace go out and fulfill his purposes for you.

Gracious God, thank you that it was in my need
that Jesus found me; that in my weakness, he
lifted me up into the shelter of his fold; and that
when I call to you in Jesus' name, you hear me and
save me from all my troubles. When I am fearful
and failing, grant me to know the immeasurable
greatness of Jesus; and may his strength, and not my
own, be the foundation for my confident obedience
of you. All this I ask in Jesus' name. Amen.

PRAY FOR LOVE

Do you know how loved you are? I have a strong suspicion that none of us do.

In a sense, our minds and our hearts will spend our whole lives catching up with the reality of the love of Christ. And so it is that Paul prays not that God would begin to love these Ephesians, but that the Ephesians would grow in their comprehension of that love. He is, he tells them, asking God…

> … *that you, being rooted and grounded in love, may have strength to comprehend with all the saints what is the breadth and length and height and depth, and to know the love of Christ that surpasses knowledge. (Ephesians 3 v 17-19)*

Paul wants them, and us, to experience the joy of knowing the unknowable—of knowing how loved we are.

How do you do that?

IT TAKES A CHURCH

First, you will not comprehend the love of God in Christ in isolation from "the saints." This is not something that happens to us on our own in our bedrooms, or on a silent retreat. The love of Christ is discovered corporately. If it takes a village to raise a child, it takes a church family to recognize how loved we are. It takes the entire family of God—the family that we've met and those that we haven't met, those that have gone before us and those that will come after us—to be able actually to get an inkling of the nature of God's love.

The family of God in Ephesus was made up of Jews and Gentiles. The family of God in the average congregation today is made up of people from different backgrounds, different ages and stages of life, different standings socially, and so on. It comprises male and female, young and old, rich and poor. We glimpse Christ's love as we sing of that love together, as we affirm it together, as we hear of it in his word together, as we encourage one another in it, as we see it displayed in each others' lives. We grow in our appreciation of his love *together*.

IT TAKES YOUR MIND AND YOUR HEART

Second, you experience it by both comprehending it with your mind and knowing it with your heart. We need to learn to think properly. One of the dangers attached to love of any notion or sort is that we immediately think in emotional terms. This then tempts us to assume that, somehow or other, our discovery of the dimensions of Christ's love will all be somewhere in our heart of hearts, and will be seen exclusively by changes in our feelings.

But no—as with every truth of the Bible, the path to our hearts leads through our minds.

Charles Simeon observed to his congregation that...

> *For the attainment of divine knowledge, we are directed to combine a dependence on God's Spirit with our own researches. Let us then not presume to separate what God has united.*
> *(Helps to Composition, page 295)*

Some of us are of the sort of bent that just wants to feel it all; others of us are of the bent that wants to research it out for ourselves. It is well worth asking yourself (or asking someone who knows you well), "Am I led more by my thoughts or my feelings? Does the road end in my head without touching my heart, or does the road short-cut to my heart without impacting my head?" The Bible engages both our thoughts and our affections, and we will have an impoverished experience of the love of Christ if it does not both engage the first and stir the second. Pray for clear thinking about how Christ loves you. And pray for stirred feelings about how Christ loves you.

IT HAS NO LIMITS

Third, the love of Christ is surprisingly comprehensive. We are used to measuring spatial objects in three dimensions. Paul comes up with four—the breadth and the length and the height and the depth. Perhaps he wants us to see that this love is so vast that it goes beyond our usual yardsticks and means of measuring.

You can find innumerable explanations for what Paul was thinking as he wrote, "breadth and length and height and depth." We shouldn't get bogged down in what we cannot know for sure. But it is interesting just to ponder for a while. Matthew Henry, in his seventeenth-century *Commentary on the Whole Bible*, wrote of these verses that...

> *the apostle designs to signify the exceeding greatness of the love of Christ ... which is higher than heaven, deeper than hell, longer than the earth, and broader than the sea.*
>
> *(Commentary on the Whole Bible)*

John Stott wrote:

> *[Christ's love] is "broad" enough to encompass all mankind ... "long" enough to last for eternity, "deep" enough to reach the most degraded sinner, and "high" enough to exalt him to heaven.*
>
> *(The Message of Ephesians, page 137)*

But perhaps most helpful is what Paul reminds us of in Philippians 2 v 5-11:

> *Christ Jesus ... though he was in the form of God, did not count equality with God a thing to be grasped, but emptied himself, by taking the form of a servant, being born in the likeness of men. And being found in human form, he humbled himself by becoming obedient to the point of death, even death*

> *on a cross. Therefore God has highly exalted him*
> *and bestowed on him the name that is above every*
> *name, so that at the name of Jesus every knee should*
> *bow, in heaven and on earth and under the earth,*
> *and every tongue confess that Jesus Christ is Lord,*
> *to the glory of God the Father.*

Christ's love is measured by contemplating the depth to which he went to secure our salvation and the height to which he was then exalted.

But whatever way we seek to try to get our heads further around the love of Christ, the main and the plain thing is surely obvious: his love is limitless, in every way.

HOW YOU CAN KNOW WHAT CAN'T BE KNOWN

This is why comprehending the love of Christ is a matter of knowing the unknowable. Paul prays that the Ephesians would "know the love of Christ that surpasses knowledge." This is a paradox, isn't it? How can you know what you can't know?! Our knowledge of the love of Christ, in our heads and our hearts, is an experiential knowledge, but it can never be an exhaustive knowledge. We cannot exhaust the knowledge of the love of Christ. There are dimensions to his love that will always remain beyond us, even as we come to appreciate more and more how vast it is.

I'm so grateful for hymn writers who manage to encapsulate theological truth in verses that are easy to memorize and lend themselves to helpful meditation: here is the best one I have found for helping us to think through what it might mean to "know the love of Christ which surpasses knowledge":

It passeth knowledge, that dear love of Thine,
My Savior, Jesus; yet this soul of mine
Would of Thy love in all its breadth and length,
Its height and depth, its everlasting strength,
Know more and more.

It passeth telling, that dear love of Thine,
My Savior, Jesus, yet these lips of mine
Would fain proclaim to sinners, far and near,
A love which can remove all guilty fear,
And love beget.

It passeth praises, that dear love of Thine,
My Savior, Jesus, yet this heart of mine
Would sing that love, so full, so rich, so free,
Which brings a rebel sinner, such as me,
Nigh unto God.

But though I cannot sing, or tell, or know
The fullness of Thy love while here below,
My empty vessel I may freely bring;
Oh thou, who art of love the living spring,
My vessel fill.

Lord Jesus, when Thee face to face I see,
When on Thy lofty throne I sit with Thee,
Then of Thy love, in all its breadth and length,
Its height and depth, its everlasting strength,
My soul shall sing.

> *(Mary Shekleton, "It Passes Knowledge,*
> *That Dear Love of Thine")*

That captures the essence of the life Paul prays for, and that we too can and should pray for. You have the provision of God to you and his love shed abroad in your heart by the Holy Spirit. You have the evidences of it, the indications of it, you see it in the lives of one another... but ultimately there's always more; and even as you enjoy this divine love, accurately describing or adequately defining it is always beyond you.

THE FULLNESS OF GOD

We cannot measure the love of Christ. But we can observe its effects. Paul prays for the Ephesian Christians to "know the love of Christ which surpasses knowledge, that you may be filled with all the fullness of God" (v 19).

This doesn't mean that we become divine; it does mean that we become the beneficiaries of all that God has promised to us in Jesus.

In his classic book *Knowing God*, J.I. Packer ties this idea of being "filled with all the fullness of God" back to Ephesians 1, where Paul talked about the fact that we have been adopted as God's sons: he "chose us in him before the foundation of the world, that we should be holy and blameless before him. In love he predestined us for adoption to himself as sons through Jesus Christ" (1 v 4-5). Packer is well worth quoting at length:

> *Adoption, by its very nature, is an act of free*
> *kindness to the person adopted. If you become a*
> *father by adopting a child, you do so because you*
> *choose to, not because you are bound to. Similarly,*
> *God adopts because he chooses to. He had no duty to*

do so. He need not have done anything about our sins save punish us as we deserve. But he loved us so; he redeemed us, forgave us, took us as his sons and daughters, and gave himself to us as our Father.

Nor does his grace stop short with that initial act, any more than the love of human parents who adopt stops short with their completing of the legal process that makes the child theirs. The establishing of the child's status as a member of the family is only a beginning. The real task remains: to establish a genuinely filial relationship between your adopted child and yourself. It is this, above all, that you want to see. Accordingly, you set yourself to win the child's love by loving. You seek to excite affection by showing affection. So with God. And throughout our life in this world, and to all eternity beyond, he will constantly be showing us, in one way or another, more and more of his love, and thereby increasing our love to him continually. The prospect before the adopted children of God is an eternity of love. (Knowing God, pages 215-216)

This is very exciting. It means that the Christian is fully, finally, irrevocably adopted by God the Father. And we will spend the whole of our lives—the whole of eternity—developing and discovering the glory of this filial relationship with the Creator. Adoption is not an end in itself; it is just the beginning.

Some of us have had fathers who let us down. Some of us, when we think about fathers, think only of disappointment or pain. But God is not an approximation of our earthly fathers. We have a heavenly Father. Even the finest moments of the best earthly fathers are only a glimpse of what this Father is to us and for us. He'll never renege on his love. He'll never leave us in the dark. He'll never forget what we told him or what he promised us. He'll make no mistakes. He'll never ditch us, even if everyone else has turned their backs on us, and no matter how much we let him down. All of us have tested his patience to limits beyond extreme. And yet still he comes again and again calling out, *My daughter. My son. You're my child. I predestined to adopt you into my family. I made you. I sought you. I bought you. I love you. I'm with you.*

There is nothing greater that can be known or heard or experienced than that this God is your Father and that you are his child—that you can say you belong to him and are loved by him, that you can know you can come to him, can run to him, can pray to him.

And this is what it means to experience the "fullness of God." We don't enjoy increasing "fullness" through some mystical experience or supposedly life-transforming spiritual rite. I've lost track of how many times people have tried to help me by suggesting that, somehow or another, what I needed to have happen to me was a kind of inward explosion; some single, definitive event. "If you will only have this happen to you… If you will only have this done to you… If you will only come up here at the end of the service and have the minister touch you…" When anyone offered that to me, I was up for it, because I wanted it. I want to know what it is to "be filled with the fullness of God." Don't you?

But the more I read my Bible, the more clearly I realize that what I need is not an inward explosion but an inward communion with God. I need the Spirit of God, through the word of God, among the people of God, to make the fatherhood of God and the love of his Son increasingly precious to me. That's how "Christ may dwell in your hearts through faith" (v 17)—it's how you can know the unknowable love, and how you can experience more "fullness of God."

There is an intimacy here—it's not something that is simply cerebral or mechanistic. It is the work of the Spirit, leading us into an ever-deepening response to God, causing us to wonder that we are God's children by adoption, bringing us to look to God as our Father, and enabling us to live as children of that Father.

GOD GAVE ME A HUG

I remember walking down the Tottenham Court Road one day in London, in a vast crowd right in the center of the city. And in a way that I have no explanation for at all, it was as though God picked me up and gave me a hug and set me back down on the Tottenham Court Road again. Later on I was talking to a friend, Joel, who's a black Pentecostal brother, and I told him, "Hey, I was walking down the Tottenham Court Road, and God hugged me." And I'll never forget his response. He laughed and said, "Well, you remember that, because he ain't gonna do it a lot."

That's not the key to fullness. It's wonderful, but it's not the key. If it were, we'd all be traveling to the Tottenham Court Road regularly, saying, "O God, could you hug me like you hugged Alistair Begg?" No—God is your Father. His Spirit lives in you. His Son loves you more than you can ever really know. So it is about experiencing a relationship. Maybe he will give you a hug. Sometimes he will give you a rebuke. Often he will speak to you through his word. Always he will give you what you need, because he's God and he's your Father. Always he will be loving you. And so we say, in the words of Frances R. Havergal's hymn:

> *O fill me with Thy fulness, Lord,*
> *Until my very heart o'erflow*
> *In kindling thought and glowing word,*
> *Thy love to tell, Thy praise to show.*
> *("O Teach Me, Lord, That I May Teach")*

That's what we are called into experiencing and enjoying, day by day. That's what we're to pray for, day by day—for ourselves, and for our brothers and sisters in our churches. Paul wanted his friends to know the unknowable love of Christ, and the intimate, fatherly closeness of God. Do you know how loved you are? It is too big fully to comprehend—but it is not too wonderful to begin to experience.

> *Father, please pour out the Spirit upon us in*
> *increased measure. Save us from paddling around*
> *in the shallows of limited vision and understanding*
> *and please sweep us up into the ocean of your*
> *matchless love. Lord, forgive me my small view of*
> *your vast generosity, and grant that every thought*

of your Fatherly care may cause my love for your Son Jesus to deepen and then overflow, so that others may be caught up in your embrace. For the sake of Jesus, in whose name I pray. Amen.

CAN ALL THIS REALLY HAPPEN?

I would like to guess what you are, at least in small measure, thinking now that you have read this far. I imagine it is something like this:

This sounds great. But it also sounds a long way from my experience. How in the world is all this supposed to happen?

How could you possibly have an understanding of God's power in your inner being? How could you really have your eyes fixed on Christ and upon eternity? How could you know God in such an intimate way? How could you be filled up with all of his fullness? How could your brothers and sisters in your church experience all those things?

We will not pray bigger, and better, if we start to give credence to the voice that doubts that any of this can really happen, and doubts that prayer really makes any difference.

So, can you make all this happen? Can you do better?

The answer in both cases is, you can't. Neither can I.

But there's a second part to the answer, and it's this: by the ministry of the Holy Spirit, you can change, as the Spirit, co-equal and co-eternal with God the Father and God the Son, goes to work to strengthen you "with power ... in your inner being" (Ephesians 3 v 16). The Christian changes as the Spirit brings home to their life, and makes real in their life, the truth concerning God.

And knowing this, and trusting this, will prove more effective in bringing us to pray bigger and better than any new resolution or new routine ever can.

We need to know the power of the Spirit.

PROOF IN THE MIRROR

If you are a Christian, to find living proof of the power of the Spirit, all you need do is go look in the mirror. It was the work of the Holy Spirit that convicted the person looking back at you of his or her sins. Many of us had decided that, yes, there were some problems in our life, but they weren't really that bad, especially compared to those of other people we knew. Most of us had concluded that if God were grading on the curve, we would be absolutely fine.

And then we began to see ourselves in a different light. We began to read the Bible, and we began to find that the Bible seemed to understand us more truly than we understood ourselves and that, in a way that we couldn't fully articulate, beyond the voice of a mere man, it was as though the very Bible itself was speaking to us. It was as though the Bible was diagnosing us; it was as though the Bible was saying, *Now this is you here, you see.*

And so when the Bible told us that "all have sinned and fall short of the glory of God" (Romans 3 v 23), rather than fighting back or walking out, we found ourselves saying, "Well, that includes me" (whereas before we might have said, "Well, that must include *them.*") This is the work of the Holy Spirit. This is the power of the Holy Spirit.

And then, realizing that we were in fact sinners in need of help, how was it that you and I were convinced that Jesus was the Savior we so desperately needed—that we could do nothing, but that he had done it all? Answer: by the same Holy Spirit, who told us, *What you need is not self-improvement, nor just to turn over a new leaf—what you need is a life-transforming encounter with the living God as your Lord and Savior.*

And that was all the work and the power of the Holy Spirit, and not yours or mine. As the nineteenth-century hymnwriter Daniel Webster Whittle put it:

> *I know not how the Spirit moves,*
> *Convincing men of sin,*
> *Revealing Jesus through the word,*
> *Creating faith in Him.*
> ("*I Know Not Why God's Wondrous Grace*")

It's miraculous; it's mysterious. And the work of the Spirit does not stop at conversion; that is just the start. The "promised Holy Spirit" is not only "the guarantee of our inheritance until we acquire possession of it"

(Ephesians 1 v 13-14); he is also the guarantee of our ongoing transformation, until we reach that inheritance. So it is the ongoing ministry of God the Holy Spirit that means that what Paul prays for the believer—for you and me—is possible.

And because it is possible, it is worth praying for.

THE SIGHTS THAT DAZZLE

If we and our churches are to grasp the love of God... if our hearts are to become fit homes for Christ... if we are to live out the hope and power given us in the gospel... we will need the Spirit to overcome our propensity to become distracted.

If you are like me, you can go through a day, two days, three days, a week, a month, before suddenly realizing you're off-course, growing distant from the gospel, growing cold to Jesus. In the words of another Victorian hymnwriter, John Ernest Bode, in "O Jesus, I Have Promised":

I see the sights that dazzle,
The tempting sounds I hear.

And those sights draw our gaze and those sounds hold our ear. How do we keep looking at Jesus and listening to Jesus? Well, it's not by someone like me saying to you, "You need to stop looking elsewhere. Just stop looking. Just stop listening. Just decide to stop." That's a good thing to do—but it won't help for very long. You'll look back, sooner or later.

No—what will really set us free is an understanding of the immensity of the riches of God's grace and glory in

Christ, because then we are so transfixed with these that the sights cease to dazzle so brightly and the sounds stop proving to be so tempting. Imagine a young man who falls in love with a girl. She captures his heart. He loves her with a passion. He writes to her (when I was young, there was still such a thing as writing a letter), and he waits with bated breath for her reply. He counts down the days and hours till he can next see her. For him, there may as well be no other girls in the world. So the others who would once have turned his head no longer do. The glances and the smiles and the kind words that would once have drawn him to another no longer do. Not because he has stopped anything, but because he has started to love someone.

So it is with us:

I see the sights that dazzle,
The tempting sounds I hear;

But, Jesus, draw Thou nearer,
And shield my soul from sin.

I thought the sights of sin would only dazzle when I was a teenager or a young man. But they still dazzle. What do I need? And how is it provided? I need to see Jesus in his glory. And that is the work of the Spirit. He can work in us to stop us being distracted, and instead be entranced by our Lord.

Some of us, though, are less distracted than we are depressed. Perhaps you feel destabilized, overwhelmed. What do you most need? Most of all, you need the glorious riches of God—his love, his hope, his peace—

which are ministered to us by the power of the Holy Spirit.

The same is true of those of us who have doubts. They can come from nowhere, can't they? What is the answer? Not a book on apologetics so much as the ministry of God's Spirit. And what about the devilish thoughts that come our way—strange and bizarre and horrible thoughts that can come while we're singing or praying or just going about our day? What is the answer? The ministry of God's Holy Spirit, pointing us back to the beauty and kindness of Jesus.

AT YOUR CORE

Can you see how utterly different this is than that counterfeit notion of Christianity as some kind of external religious effort whereby we try to attach outward behaviors to ourselves, that we think will make us acceptable to God and impressive to others? That is a dead-end street, because it relies on your own efforts—your own power to will change in your life. That's not Christianity. Christianity is about the work of the Spirit to call you, convert you, and change you. That starts not skin-deep but heart-deep—or, as Paul puts it, "in your inner being" (Ephesians 3 v 16).

This is the deep center of who you are. It's your core, your heart. Essentially Paul is dealing in a spiritual way with what has become common parlance in physical exercise. What matters in fitness and in sports technique is your core. A strong core is the reason why top golfers are able to hit the ball so far. It's not about their biceps but their core. And what Paul is saying is that the same thing is true spiritually; it's the core that God is interested in and goes to work on because it's the foundation of everything you are and all that you do. It's the part of you that isn't obvious to people; it's the real you. It's you on your own, it's you in your bedroom, it's you in your car, and it's the part of you that lasts forever.

Of course our outer selves—our bodies, with all of their functions and its faculties—is important. But they are not all-important, or even most important. Yet Western culture is fixated on the outer self—how I look, what I have, where I live, what I do, what I earn, how significant I am. That's one reason why our culture cannot understand the kind of change the Spirit brings, nor recognize the extent of the divine power that such change requires—because it's in the "inner being." Paul is saying that the Spirit's power is at work in our inner selves. This is why the Christian can, with Paul, say that the outer self is wasting away (and, at my age, the evidence of this truth is plain every time I try to get out of bed in the morning), but yet we are rejoicing, because we are being inwardly renewed (2 Corinthians 4 v 16).

It's why death need hold no fear for the Christian. As the great American evangelist D.L. Moody put it, according to his biographers Paul Dwight Moody and Arthur Percy Fitt:

> *One day you will read in the papers that D.L. Moody, of East Northfield, is dead. Don't you believe a word of it! At that moment I shall be more alive than I am now.*
>
> *(The Shorter Life of D.L. Moody, Vol. 1, page 9)*

He was talking about the inner man: the real him. That's where the Spirit goes to work. And, though his work is spiritual and deep, he uses means to fulfill his purpose, so that Christ may dwell in our hearts through faith, so that we might be filled with all the fullness of God. And the means that God uses to complete his purposes are these: preaching, prayer, fellowship and the proper use of the sacraments.

I meet many people who are disenchanted with the Christian life, and who complain that they see none of the joy and excitement within themselves that the Bible seems to hold out to the Christian. My questions are always these: "Are you listening attentively and expectantly to good Bible preaching? Are you engaging meaningfully in fellowship with others in your church? Have you been baptized, and are you coming to the Lord's Table to share his supper in a careful, thoughtful way? Are you praying?"

Almost always, the answer to at least one of those questions is no. And the truth is that when we choose to reject God's chosen means by which the Spirit works, then we ought not to be surprised if we discover in our lives an absence of the strengthening power for which Paul prays. If we neglect the means, we miss out on the provision.

HE IS ABLE

All this explains why Paul does not say to the Ephesians, *I am just going to preach to you, because if you are motivated enough, you'll be able to enjoy a life of gospel peace and security and love and growth.*

No. He says, *I am going to pray for you, for God is able to bring you into this experience. I'm going to pray for you, because in prayer I am speaking to "him who is able to do far more abundantly than all that we ask or think" (Ephesians 3 v 20).*

And the language here is just piled up—encouragement on top of encouragement. God is able—able to do what we ask. He is able—able to do what we think of asking but aren't sure that we can. He is able—able to do far more than we even thought of asking. There is nothing you can ask for, or think of asking for, about which he does not say, *I am able to do better than that.*

You get the point? He is able.

So the encouragement (and the command) is to come to God and ask him for big things. I was reflecting on this verse, and it made me think, "I believe in the living God, who is able to do far more abundantly than all that anyone can ask or even imagine. What am I asking God for? How big are my prayers, and how big are my prayers for my church?" We sin when we think God's power is limited or doubt his willingness to display his power. Small prayers betray a suspicion that we have a small God. We don't. He is able to do immeasurably more than you can imagine.

So, ask him. Ask as Paul did. Not for health and wealth and happiness, as though, if you dig in here, you'll be able to get your home in the Bahamas and the personal jet. No, ask him for bigger things than that—to be filled with his fullness, to be able to grasp the unknowable love of Christ, to live for the treasures of your future inheritance. And ask for those things for the Christians you know, too—those who encourage you, and those who try your patience and discourage your spirit. If God is able to change you, he'll certainly be able to change them!

How is all this that Paul prays for, and that God wants us to pray for, supposed to happen? According to the power that is at work within us. Not ours, but his. And he is able. Pray like that's true.

Father in heaven, I thank you for the gift of prayer. Even though there are some things that are a mystery to me, I know that this is a necessity—and I exercise the privilege fully confident in both your ability and willingness to do far more than I could ever imagine or guess. Help me to ask then for big things, for the sake of your glory and through your matchless power. Enable me to pray big. For Jesus' sake. Amen.

EPILOGUE:
WHO WE PRAY FOR

As we finish our time together in this short book, let me ask you this: who do you pray for?

I think we should have three sorts of people in mind when, spiritually speaking, we get onto our knees and say, "Dearest Father..."

FOR YOUR SAKE

First is the most obvious one (and certainly the one that comes most naturally): ourselves. We are to pray for ourselves. We need to pray for ourselves, for humans are dependent beings. The Lord Jesus himself prayed in thanks for what his Father had done for and in and through him:

> Jesus ... lifted up his eyes to heaven, and said,
> "Father, the hour has come; glorify your Son that
> the Son may glorify you, since you have given him
> authority over all flesh, to give eternal life to all
> whom you have given him. And this is eternal life,

that they know you, the only true God, and Jesus
Christ whom you have sent. I glorified you on
earth, having accomplished the work that you gave
me to do. And now, Father, glorify me in your own
presence with the glory that I had with you before the
world existed. (John 17 v 1-5)

And Jesus also asked God to do things for him:

He withdrew from [the disciples] about a stone's
throw, and knelt down and prayed, saying,
"Father, if you are willing, remove this cup from
me. Nevertheless, not my will, but yours, be done."
And there appeared to him an angel from heaven,
strengthening him. And being in agony he prayed
more earnestly; and his sweat became like great
drops of blood falling down to the ground.
(Luke 22 v 41-44)

Do you pray for yourself? Not for your health and wealth—not for an easy day or a promotion at work or respect from your kids—but for bigger things? How might your prayer life be transformed if you used the headings of this book to shape your prayers for your own heart and mind and lips and hands?

FOR THEIR SAKE

Second, we can learn from the focus of Paul's prayers in Ephesians—those around us. Don't forget where Paul was as he wrote—in confinement in Rome. He may well have been chained to a soldier; at best he was under a form of house arrest, with no freedom to come and go as he pleased. Our prayers reveal our priorities and our pre-occupations; and as we listen in on Paul, we realize that his focus is on those who have become the objects of his concern and of his affection. It is on others.

Paul prays for those he knows and loves who do not know and love Christ and eternal life through him: speaking of his Jewish relatives and countrymen, he tells the Roman church, "Brothers, my heart's desire and prayer to God for them is that they may be saved" (Romans 10 v 1).

And, as we've seen, Paul pours out his soul to God for those believers to whom he writes, just as his Master did and does for his people (John 17 v 9-11, 15-16, 24; Hebrews 7 v 25). In his imprisonment, Paul was not consumed with agitating for his release, nor were his prayers centered on asking for his release. He wrote Ephesians, Philippians, Colossians, Galatians, and Philemon while he was in this imprisonment. And he prayed—constantly prayed—and his prayers surrounded the churches to whom he wrote. He prayed big, spiritual, ambitious prayers for them. His legs may have been chained but his heart was free to pray, and pray he did.

This is a great reminder to us. It is always good to be praying more for others than for ourselves. In our selfie-obsessed culture, praying this way reminds us that we are not the center of the world, and that our needs are not necessarily the most pressing in our churches. There is no one who does not need your prayers: even the apostle knew he needed others to be in prayer for him, as he told the Ephesian church to "keep alert with all perseverance, making supplication for all the saints, and also for me, that words may be given to me in opening my mouth boldly to proclaim the mystery of the gospel" (Ephesians 6 v 18-19).

Paul's prison prayers also remind us that in those seasons when we are not able to do all that we would like to, or serve in all the ways that we used to, we can pray; and time spent in prayer is never time wasted. The evil one loves to come to believers and say, "You know, all your best days are behind you; you've got nothing really to contribute anymore." Don't listen to him for a moment. You can always pray. Whenever a person professes faith in Jesus Christ... whenever the cause of the gospel is advanced... whenever a work of great transformation takes place in a believer... you will find that it is directly tied to the prayers of the people of God. This prayer usually goes unseen in this world, but it is seen by God, it brings pleasure to God, and it will one day be rewarded by God (Matthew 6 v 6).

Will you pray for others? For their salvation and their sanctification? How might your prayer life be transformed if you used the headings of this book to shape your prayers for your family, your church family, and your neighbors?

FOR HIS SAKE

The third person for whose sake we pray is the One who is in focus at the end of Paul's prayer in Ephesians 3:

Now to him who is able to do far more abundantly than all that we ask or think, according to the

*power at work within us, to him be glory in
the church and in Christ Jesus throughout all
generations, forever and ever. Amen. (3 v 20-21)*

We are praying, first and foremost, for the glory of God. Paul closes his prayer with a doxology—theologically informed praise of God. He finishes by praying that God would get the glory he deserves. He is the God who is perfect, powerful, and infinitely, eternally praiseworthy. Yes, Paul is asking God to do all these glorious things for the Christians in Ephesus for their sakes—but supremely, Paul is asking God to do it for God's sake. For, just as God's glory was, is, and will be revealed "in Christ Jesus," so his glory is seen "in the church."

What does that mean? It means that the communicable attributes of God—those qualities in God's character which he also works to grow in his people—are displayed through his people. His love and his faithfulness and his compassion and his goodness and his forgiveness and so on can be and should be seen in his church, so that throughout all of the ages in the church of Jesus Christ, men and women will encounter the glory of God. God's glory—his perfections which are invisible—are made visible in the transformation that he has brought about in the lives of ordinary, redeemed men and women.

This glory is meant to become tangible to people when they encounter a church. People are supposed to say:

*"Oh, I think people in here love people. They
actually love me. I'm surprised, because I'm used
to people giving me the elbow, but that was*

interesting. And you know, when I hung around with them for a little while, I discovered that there was a kind of forgiving spirit about these people. In fact, there was almost an empathetic compassion about them.

"Not only that, but I noticed that they weren't all the same. They didn't all come from the same background. They didn't all have the same intelligence quotient. They didn't all have the same color of skin. They weren't all coming from the same career sectors or the same communities. But that didn't seem to matter. In fact, they celebrated it."

When someone can say that, God's glory is being manifested in his church. In Ephesus, as Jewish Christians and Gentile Christians—called by God from cultures and identities that hated each other and were raised to be deeply suspicious of each other—met and sang and ate and prayed together, God's glory—his power to transform, and his perfect compassion and love—was being displayed.

When a church is gripped by God's grace—when its members focus their heart-eyes on Jesus and on eternity; when the buffeting of circumstances doesn't shake their hope, and they live for the riches of knowing God rather than the fleeting treasures of this world; when they look to and live out of a power greater than themselves—then the glory of God is revealed in the Bride, just as it is in the Bridegroom. When that grace takes hold of a church community, then the world looks on and says, "That is at least worth investigating." And then we're able to tell them that this Lord Jesus Christ is a king who will reign forever and forever.

And then God's name is praised.

So we pray big prayers. We pray like Paul. We pray for our own sake, for we are dependent creatures and we need the help of the God who is able to do what we are quite unable to do. We pray for the sake of others, because what they most need from us is our prayers. And, most of all, we pray for God's sake: that the God who made us and died for us and rose for us and rules for us and will return to us might be glorified in our lives and in our churches.

To him who is able to do far more abundantly than all that we ask or think, according to the power at work within us, to him be glory in the church and in Christ Jesus throughout all generations, forever and ever. Amen.

BIBLIOGRAPHY

Matthew Henry, *Commentary on the Whole Bible* (available at ccel.org)

Herman Hoeksma, "The Doctrine of the Church, Chapter III, The Attributes and Marks of the Church (Continued)" in *The Standard Bearer*, Vol. 40, Issue 2 (October 15th, 1963)

Henry Martyn, *Journals and Letters of the Rev. Henry Martyn, B.D.*, Vol. 1, ed. S. Wilberforce (R.B. Seeley and W. Burnside, 1838)

Paul Dwight Moody and Arthur Percy Fitt, *The Shorter Life of D.L. Moody*, Vol. 1 (The Bible Institute Colportage Associaton, 1900)

J.I. Packer, *Knowing God* (IVP USA, 1973: reprinted 2018)

Joe Queenan, *Balsamic Dreams* (Henry Holt and Company, 2002)

Charles Simeon, *Helps to Composition, or, Five Hundred Skeletons of Sermons*, Vol. 1, Pt. 1 (John Burges, 1901)

Charles H. Spurgeon, *Letters to My Students,* Vol. 1 (Passmore and Alabaster, 1875)

Charles H. Spurgeon, *The New Park Street Pulpit*, Vol. 1 (available at www.spurgeon.org)

John Stott, *The Message of Ephesians* in The Bible Speaks Today Commentary Series (IVP UK, 1979)

thegoodbook
COMPANY

BIBLICAL | RELEVANT | ACCESSIBLE

At The Good Book Company, we are dedicated to helping Christians and local churches grow. We believe that God's growth process always starts with hearing clearly what he has said to us through his timeless word—the Bible.

Ever since we opened our doors in 1991, we have been striving to produce Bible-based resources that bring glory to God. We have grown to become an international provider of user-friendly resources to the Christian community, with believers of all backgrounds and denominations using our books, Bible studies, devotionals, evangelistic resources, and DVD-based courses.

We want to equip ordinary Christians to live for Christ day by day, and churches to grow in their knowledge of God, their love for one another, and the effectiveness of their outreach.

Call us for a discussion of your needs or visit one of our local websites for more information on the resources and services we provide.

Your friends at The Good Book Company

thegoodbook.com | thegoodbook.co.uk
thegoodbook.com.au | thegoodbook.co.nz
thegoodbook.co.in